CULTURE
in Thailand

Melanie Guile

www.heinemann.co.uk/library

Visit our website to find out more information about Heinemann Library books.

To order:

☎ Phone 44 (0) 1865 888066

▤ Send a fax to 44 (0) 1865 314091

💻 Visit the Heinemann Bookshop at www.heinemann.co.uk/library to browse our catalogue and order online.

First published 2003 in Australia by Heinemann
Library a division of Harcourt Education Australia,
18–22 Salmon Street, Port Melbourne Victoria 3207
Australia (a division of Reed International Books
Australia Pty Ltd, ABN 70 001 002 357).

Series cover and text design by Stella Vassiliou
Paged by Stella Vassiliou
Edited by Carmel Heron
Production by Michelle Sweeney

Pre-press by Digital Imaging Group (DIG),
Melbourne, Australia
Printed and bound in China by WKT Company
Ltd.

ISBN 1 74070 132 1 (hardback)
08 07 06 05 04 03
10 9 8 7 6 5 4 3 2 1

ISBN 0 431 18129 2 (paperback)
09 08 07 06 05
10 9 8 7 6 5 4 3 2 1

British Library Cataloguing in Publication Data

Guile, Melanie.
Culture in Thailand.
306'.09593
A full catalogue record for this book is available from
the British library.

Acknowledgements

Cover photograph of Buddhist monks making flower
offerings at Phra Phutthabat Temple in Saraburi
Province, supplied by AP/AAP/Sakchai Lalit ©
2002, The Associated Press.

Other photographs supplied by: AFP/AAP/Romeo
Gacad: pp. 11, 22; AP/AAP/Sakchai Lalit © 2002,
The Associated Press: pp. 8, 10, 19; Australian Picture
Library (APL)/Corbis/© AFP: pp. 4, 9 (top), /©
Bohemian Nomad Picturemakers: p. 12, /© Jack
Fields: p. 20, /© Michael Freeman: p. 23, /© Lindsay
Hebberd: pp. 13, 28, /© John Hulme & Eye
Ubiquitous: p. 16, /© Luca I. Tettoni: p. 26;
BOONMA, Montien, Thailand 1953–2000,
Terracotta, gilded wood, 300 x 350 x 300cm
(approx.), The Kenneth and Yasuko Myer Collection
of Contemporary Asian Art. Purchased 1993 with
funds from The Myer Foundation, Michael Simcha
Baevski, and Ann Gamble Myer through the
Queensland Art Gallery Foundation. Reproduced by
permission, from the collection of the Queensland
Art Gallery, Brisbane: p. 27; Lonely Planet
Images/Lee Foster: p. 7; Tourism Authority of
Thailand: pp. 9 (bottom), 14, 15, 17, 18, 29;
www.bbbird.com: p. 21; www.IMDB.com: p. 25.

Every attempt has been made to trace and
acknowledge copyright. Where an attempt has been
unsuccessful, the publisher would be pleased to hear
from the copyright owner so any omission or error
can be rectified. in subsequent printings

CONTENTS

Words that appear in bold, **like this**, are explained in the glossary on page 30.

CULTURE IN
Thailand

Cultural crossroads

Thailand lies among a rich mix of Asian countries and cultures. Burma, Laos and Cambodia fan out around it in the north, and Malaysia borders it at the south end of its long **peninsula**. China is Thailand's north–eastern neighbour and India lies across the Andaman Sea to the west. Many **ethnic** tribal groups live in the hills in the north and their distinctive ways of life add variety to Thailand's vibrant cultural mix.

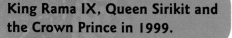

King Rama IX, Queen Sirikit and the Crown Prince in 1999.

The longest reign

King Bhumibol Adulyadej (also called Rama IX) came to the throne in 1946 and is the world's longest-reigning monarch. His wife is Queen Sirikit. The country is governed by an elected **parliament** and the king gives advice but has no power to rule. Thai kings traditionally had god-like status, and Thais still have great love and respect for the royal family. Teenage girls post pictures of the royal family on their personal websites, and everyone stands to attention for the national anthem ('Hymn of praise for the King') before every film show.

Thailand has absorbed many foreign influences, while also honouring its own traditions. Some forms of Thai literature, dance and music have roots in India; Chinese pottery, painting and weaving influenced many Thai **artisans**; Malay people introduced shadow puppetry, and hill tribespeople brought metalworking techniques. Yet the Thais have added their own skills and style to these traditions and created a remarkable and **diverse** culture that is quite different from any other.

What is culture?

Culture is a people's way of living. It is the way in which people identify themselves as a group, separate and different from any other. Culture includes a group's spoken and written language, social customs and habits, as well as its traditions of art, craft, dance, drama, music, literature and religion.

4

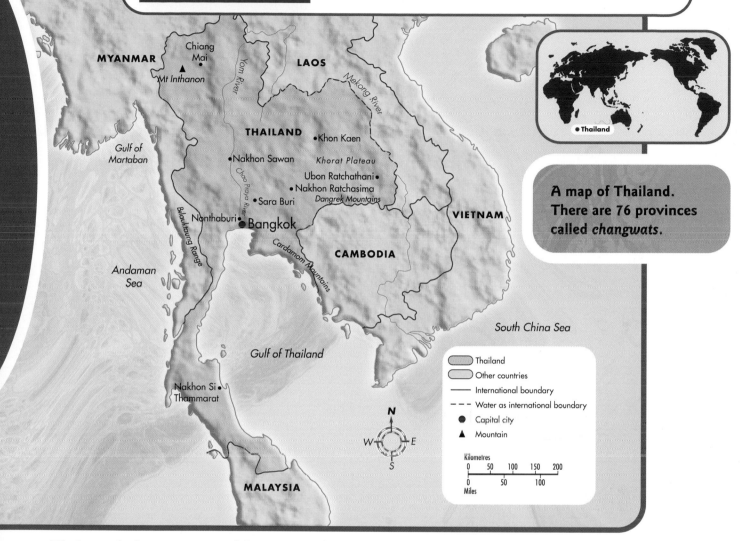

The wide blue band in the middle represents royal power, the two white bands stand for the purity of **Buddhism** and the red bands represent the blood of the Thai people. The flag was designed by King Rama VI in 1917.

A map of Thailand. There are 76 provinces called *changwats*.

MYANMAR
Chiang Mai
Mt Inthanon
Yom River
LAOS
Mekong River
THAILAND
Khon Kaen
Nakhon Sawan
Khorat Plateau
Ubon Ratchathani
Chao Praya River
Nakhon Ratchasima
Sara Buri
Dangrek Mountains
Nonthaburi
Bangkok
VIETNAM
Gulf of Martaban
Bilauktaung Range
Cardamom Mountains
CAMBODIA
Andaman Sea
South China Sea
Gulf of Thailand
Nakhon Si Thammarat
MALAYSIA

● Thailand

Thailand
Other countries
International boundary
Water as international boundary
● Capital city
▲ Mountain

Kilometres
0 50 100 150 200
0 50 100
Miles

N
W E
S

Thai people have great confidence in their traditions and their way of life. They are not threatened by new ideas, and have freely adopted modern, international ways of doing things. Yet traditions are still a vital part of Thai people's lives – the old and the new exist comfortably side by side.

Both young and old people still consult fortune-tellers in times of trouble. Floating offerings of candles and flowers at the Festival of Lights are now made with **polystyrene** foam. Buddhist practices are widely respected – the government gives young men three months paid leave for their traditional time of prayer and contemplation as monks. Thai values of personal **restraint**, modesty and politeness are strong in spite of western influences.

Living conditions

Living standards in Thailand have improved rapidly in the last 30 years, especially in the cities, but there is a large gap between rich and poor. The wealthy live in modern houses in major cities like Bangkok and Chiang Mai, drive new cars and enjoy dance clubs, films and fancy restaurants. **Rural** people (around 68 per cent of the population) earn up to ten times less than city dwellers, and eke out a living as farmers. Yet government education and health systems have improved poor people's lives.

Nine years of schooling is **compulsory** and 94 per cent of people can read and write, which is one of the best literacy rates in Asia. Health care is quite good with a life expectancy of around 70 years, but **AIDS** is a serious problem.

An independent nation

Thailand has been an independent nation since 1238 when the Thai people drove out the Khmers (modern-day Cambodians) and established their own state. Until 1939 Thailand was known as Siam. *Thai* means free so Thailand means 'Land of the free'. The country's 62.1 million people are very proud of the fact that Thailand is the only country in the region that has never been **colonised** by European powers. Thais were able to keep their independence through careful, friendly dealings with powerful *farang* (foreigners).

Cultural mix

The Thais form around 82 per cent of the population and have several sub-groups: the northern Thais, the Thai Pak Tai in the south, the Thai Lao in the north-east, and the Central Thais who live on the fertile central plains of the Chao Praya river valley. Each group has its own **dialect** and customs, but the Central Thais are the **dominant** culture, and their dialect is the official language of Thailand.

Language

The official language of Thailand is also called Thai. Spoken Thai belongs to the **Tai** group of languages brought to Thailand long ago by people from Southern China. It has no links with any other languages. In spoken Thai, different voice tones (low, high, level, rising, falling) change the meaning of a word. For example, *ma* can mean 'horse', 'dog' or 'come', depending on the tone. Written Thai is very complicated; there are no spaces between words, and the letters have special signs surrounding them that indicate the tone.

The Thais live peacefully with the many other **ethnic groups** in the country, including the people of the northern hill tribes (around 2 per cent), the Malays (3.5 per cent) in the far south, Chinese people (12 per cent) and the **indigenous** sea gypsies (fewer than 1 per cent).

Environment

Thailand has some of the world's great **hardwood** forests. It is also rich in minerals (gold, tin, oil) and hosts over 9 million tourists each year. All this means growing wealth for the country, and average incomes in 1997 were 19 times greater than they were in 1963. But it also means problems for the environment. Logging has damaged many forests. Resorts have forever changed Thailand's magnificent coasts and islands. Bangkok's air and water are badly polluted. For many years, particularly during the 1980s and 1990s, **corrupt** government officials turned a blind eye to polluters in return for bribes of money. But recently the situation has improved. It is now illegal to log or export any of Thailand's hardwoods, and the government passed a law in 1992 that sets aside 79 national parks, 89 non-hunting zones and 35 forest reserves for **conservation**.

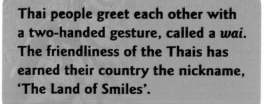

Thai people greet each other with a two-handed gesture, called a *wai*. The friendliness of the Thais has earned their country the nickname, 'The Land of Smiles'.

Land of smiles

Thai people have a reputation for friendliness, openness and **tolerance** of difference. The millions of foreign tourists (*farang*) who come through their country every year are generally welcomed in the tradition of *nam-jai* (kindness and helpfulness). It may take the form of offers of lifts or a bed, paying for meals, or going out of the way to help a stranger.

Buddhism

Ninety-five per cent of Thai people follow the **Buddhist** religion, which was brought to Thailand in the 1200s from Sri Lanka. Basic beliefs include reincarnation (being reborn) and the law of *karma*, by which good deeds earn **merit** for the next life. Harmony, tolerance and avoiding harm to others are important values. Followers give donations to monks and make offerings at Buddhist shrines. Caged birds are often sold outside temples so worshippers can gain merit by setting them free.

Buddhist monks during *Phansa* **(also called Buddhist Lent or Rains Retreat).**

Don't complain

In Thai culture, it is not considered polite to make a fuss about anything wrong. An often-repeated saying is *mai pen rai*, which means something like 'don't worry, it's nothing'. To disagree, criticise or get angry is considered shameful and embarrassing, and conflict is to be avoided. Self-control and politeness are a vital part of 'saving face' – both your own and other people's. This makes for smooth social relations, but it can also have less positive effects. Some people believe that Thailand's social troubles, such as government **corruption**, will never improve because its citizens are too reluctant to complain about the problems they see.

Becoming a monk

Most Thai men are expected to become Buddhist monks for a short period. Many join the priesthood during the three months of *Phansa* (Rains Retreat). A family gains great respect when a son becomes a monk. Traditionally, three months is the minimum stay in the monastery, but today, two weeks is acceptable. Women traditionally have not become monks, but the first was ordained in 2002.

A water fight during *Songkran*, or Thai New Year.

Flickering candles are set afloat at the beautiful *Loi Kratong* (Festival of Lights).

Manners

Ideal behaviour in Thai culture is traditionally dignified, modest (in dress and behaviour) and quiet. Loud, bold gestures or speech are considered rude. It is also rude to point your foot at anyone, even when sitting on the floor, or to reach for anything using your left hand. Social **status** often dictates the way Thai people behave towards one another. The *phuu nawy* (small person) shows respect for the *phuu yai* (big person), who in turn is expected to protect the *phuu nawy*. Bosses, teachers, older people and parents generally are honoured as *phuu yai*.

Festivals and holidays

Religious rituals and holy days are important to the devoutly Buddhist Thais, but they also know how to have fun.

New Years' celebrations

People joke that only fun-loving Thais celebrate three new years – the European (in January), the Chinese (January or February) and the traditional Thai New Year, *Songkran* (around 13 April). This ancient rain ceremony involves temple visits, ritual washing of **Buddha** statues and paying respect to elders by pouring perfumed water over their hands and receiving blessings from them. But its main feature today is water fights, and everyone has great fun getting drenched.

Festival of Lights

Held under a full moon in November or December, *Loi Kratong* is an ancient and beautiful festival to honour the water spirits. People make little boats (*kratong*) with offerings of a lighted candle, incense, flowers and coins, and set them afloat in canals and rivers. Each offering holds a wish. If the candle stays alight, it is granted. In Chiang Mai, a city in northern Thailand, they call this festival *Yi Peng*, and fly masses of hot-air paper lanterns in a brilliant display. The festival includes a parade of huge floats, ending at the river where people release offerings into the water.

Royal Ploughing Ceremony

For over 2500 years the Royal Ploughing Ceremony has marked the start of rice planting season. This very formal ceremony was originally a **Hindu** fertility **ritual**. It is held in May in Sanam Luang in front of the Grand Palace in the presence of the king. White buffalo decorated with flowers pull a red and gold plough in a procession with brilliantly costumed attendants. Traditional music is played with drums and **conch shell** trumpets. Four priestesses carry gold and silver baskets of rice, which is scattered on the ground. The bulls are offered seven different foods and drinks. Whichever they choose predicts the quality of the harvest.

Rains Retreat

The three-month period starting mid-July to mid-August called *Phansa* (also called Buddhist Lent or the Rains Retreat) marks a time of reflection and prayer for **Buddhist** monks, who retreat to their *wat* (monastery). *Phansa* follows the great celebration of **Buddha's** Birthday called *Visakha Puja* (Wesak Day), held in May or June, and the celebration of *Asalaha Puja* (Buddha's first sermon after his enlightenment), which ushers in *Phansa*. During these holy days, people make offerings of food and robes to the monks as good deeds to gain **merit** for the next life.

The Royal Ploughing Ceremony is an ancient ritual held to ensure a good rice harvest.

Sport and leisure

Thai people make the most of their leisure time and enjoy many traditional sports and games. These are often played with much laughter in a spirit of fun – or *sanuk*, as the Thais call it.

Thai boxing

Muay thai, Thailand's traditional form of boxing, dates from the 1400s. The sport involves quick, sharp movements, striking with elbows, feet and hands. A ritual dance called *ram muay* is performed before each bout. Boxers are trained from an early age and often have professional fights by the age of ten. Thailand's most famous boxer was Khaosai Galaxy who went on to be world champion **welterweight** from 1984–1990.

Traditional games

Another traditional sport is *takro*, a game where players have to keep a ball in the air using feet, elbows and head but not the hands. Several players compete to try to put the ball through a ring or over a net. *Takro* is very popular today and is played in the Asian Games sports competitions.

Thais also enjoy a kite-flying game in which two teams compete – one with a large, star-shaped kite (*chula*), and the other with a diamond-shaped kite (*pakpao*). Each team tries to bring the other team's kite down. The *chula* (called the male kite) has bamboo hooks on the tail to grip the female *pakpao*, which has a loop to snare the *chula*.

The Thai and Malaysian teams playing *takro* at the 14th Asian Games in 2002.

The Central Thai are the main **ethnic group** in Thailand, but there are many smaller groups, including Thai sub-groups, the Chinese, Malays, sea gypsies and many hill tribes in the north. People of the hill tribes live in remote mountain villages in north-east Thailand and do not enjoy a high standard of living. Most are farmers, but supplement their income by selling handcrafts and hosting tourists. They have held on to their beliefs, customs and traditional ways, and are particularly famous for their brilliantly coloured costumes, which attract tourists from around the world.

Good neighbours

Chinese businessmen came to Thailand over 200 years ago as traders and became rich merchants in the country's booming ports. Most married into Thai families to produce a prosperous Chinese–Thai culture, which still thrives in the port cities. In contrast to the **Buddhist** Thais, Malay people are **Muslim**. They are concentrated in the four southernmost provinces: Satun, Songkhla, Yala and Narathiwat, which are strongly Muslim in culture.

A Karen woman wearing the traditional red and pink clothes of a married woman.

The Karen

The Karen people have farmed in the foothills along the Thai–Burmese border for over 200 years. Of Tibetan/Burmese origin, they are the largest of the hill tribes, with a population of over 300 000. Their small bamboo houses are built on stilts with pens for domestic animals (pigs, chickens and buffalo) underneath. Traditionally, Karen worshipped **ancestor** spirits, but many are now Christian. Thousands have fled discrimination in Burma and live in huge refugee camps on the Thai and Cambodian borders. Women, not men, **inherit** property in Karen society. They are famous for the beauty and skill of their weaving, fabric dyeing and cross-stitch embroidery.

The Hmong

The Hmong came to northern Thailand from southern China over the past 100 years, fleeing from war and unrest. Many sub-groups exist among the 60 000-strong population, including the Blue Hmong, the White Hmong and the Black Hmong, named after the main colours used in their traditional costumes. They farm and also sell crafts and textiles. The men are known for their metalwork skill and the women for their beautiful weaving and embroidery.

The Akha

The Akha people came from Tibet in 1911 to live in Chiang Rai and Chiang Mai provinces. They are deeply religious people who follow the *akhazhan* (the *Akha* way of life) – a set of beliefs which they believe will guide them to good fortune. They are farmers who prefer high mountain places and build houses on low stilts with steeply pitched roofs. Each Akha village has a sacred gateway carved and decorated with human objects like weapons, tools and vehicles dedicated to the guardian spirits. At the famous Swinging Festival each August, the villagers take turns to use a large swing. The meaning of this ancient festival is lost, but it provides great fun for the villagers. Like other hill tribes, the Akha are famous for their costumes, and make money at markets from their crafts.

Sea gypsies

In the islands and bays along the south-west coast live the *chao naam* or **indigenous** sea gypsies. These expert seafarers are **nomadic** Muslim people who roam the Andaman Sea coast, fishing and diving for shellfish on the coral reefs. With stones strapped to their waist to weigh them down, and an air tube to breathe through, they are said to be able to dive to 60 metres. Their traditional culture is under great pressure from coastal tourist development, which deprives them of fishing grounds.

COSTUME
and clothing

A reputation for elegance

Thai people have long had a reputation for fine fabrics and elegant clothing. Silk, **hemp** and cotton cloth fragments have been found in 5000-year-old tombs in north-east Thailand, and this area is still the country's largest producer of spun and woven silk. Today, there are two main kinds of traditional costume – that of the Central Thais (the largest **ethnic group**), and the folk costumes of the many different hill tribes who live in the mountainous north of the country.

National dress

In 1960, Queen Sirikit had a number of traditional costumes designed for her to wear on a world tour, and these costumes have become accepted as the national dress. It consists of an ankle-length, wrap-around skirt, called a *pasin* or *phasin*, made of Thai silk with a decorated hem. A three-quarter or short-sleeved, collarless blouse with five front buttons sits over the *pasin*. A long embroidered sash is often worn draped over one shoulder. Women wear make-up and accessories including jewelled belts, upper armbands and necklaces. The effect is sleek, slim, elegant and very stylish.

Men wear dark trousers and a straight shirt called a *seua phra ratchathan* with a high collarless neck. The shirt sits on the hips and is sometimes worn with a wide waist sash. Today, most Thai people wear western-style clothing, and put on traditional costume only on special occasions.

The elegant Thai traditional costume.

Folk costumes

Tribal groups in north-eastern Thailand are famous for their costumes, which are still in daily use. From early childhood, girls learn to spin, weave, dye, sew and embroider. Unlike the Central Thais, women of the hill tribes cover their hair with turbans and do not wear make-up. Silver coins, chains and jewellery are very popular, and each tribal group wears its own distinct colours, designs and decorations.

Akha costume

The Akha people are famous for their dazzling headdresses. The women's costume consists of striped leggings, a short black skirt with a white beaded apron and a loose black jacket with embroidered cuffs. The headdress is a cone made of bamboo, and covered with beads, silver studs, seeds, green beetle wings, horsehair tassels and monkey fur. The front is fringed with silver coins. Tassels made of red-dyed chicken feathers and woollen pompoms dangle down the back.

Hmong traditional dress

There are two main Hmong groups – the Hmong Deaw (White Hmong) and the Hmong Njua (literally Green but commonly called the Blue Hmong) – plus many sub-groups, all of them renowned for their sewing, weaving and embroidery skills. Blue Hmong women wear a black top with a full, pleated short skirt with bands of **batik** and cross-stitch embroidery. They bind their waists with lengths of blue material to create a rounded figure, and add a bright pink or red sash tied at the back, plus several belts decorated with silver coins. They also wear elaborate headdresses and many strands of silver necklaces. The men wear baggy black pants drawn tight at the ankles, embroidered black shirts and black skullcaps.

Akha women in traditional dress. Akha headdresses are especially elaborate and beautiful.

The long-necked people

The Padaung (a sub-group of the Karen people) are known as the long-necked people because the women wear many tight, thick brass rings around their necks. Over many years, their necks stretch, which is considered a sign of beauty among the Padaung. A traditional punishment for women was to remove the rings. This can be fatal because the neck becomes weakened and the women cannot hold up their heads without the rings. Younger women are reluctant to accept the rings, so the practice is dying out.

FOOD

Fresh and tasty

Thai food is famous for its freshness, variety and spicy taste. It combines the cooking styles of many nearby cultures including Indian, southern Chinese, Vietnamese, Malay and Khmer (Cambodian). Portuguese traders also left their mark in the egg dishes enjoyed by Thai people. Thai cuisine uses fresh ingredients and cooks food lightly, often steaming, boiling or stir-frying it. Lots of vegetables are cooked with pork, beef, chicken, duck, fish and other seafood, and served with rice or sometimes noodles made of wheat. Thais do not eat dairy foods or lamb, and **Muslims** in the southern provinces do not eat pork because their religion forbids it.

Rice

Rice (*khao*) is the staple or basic food eaten all over Thailand, either steamed, or fried with morsels of meat or seafood. In the north, sticky rice (*khao niao*) is served in bamboo baskets and eaten with the fingers. Elsewhere, rice is eaten with a spoon called a *chon*. Thai people also use a fork (*som*) for serving food (but never for eating). One of Thailand's most popular dishes is *khao niao mamuang*, which is sliced mangoes with rice cooked in coconut milk. Rice is also made into flour and used in many recipes.

Street stalls like this one provide delicious snacks in city areas.

Good manners

Traditionally, Thai people eat sitting on the floor at a low table. All dishes are placed in the centre of the table and each person helps themself to what they want. It is the custom to start each meal with a spoonful of rice on its own. If you are a guest, it is polite to leave some food on your plate to show that your host provided more than you could eat.

Carved fruit and vegetables are used for decoration on special occasions and festival days.

Spicy fare

A large number of spices and herbs are used to add zest to dishes, including garlic, coriander, lime, lemon grass, ginger, pepper and chilli. Thai curries are often fiery hot, particularly in the south. A yellow fish curry called *kaeng tai plaa* is said to be the hottest of all. Coconut milk is used in curries, sauces and sweets, and fish sauce or shrimp paste add a salty tang to many dishes. Thailand's most famous dish is a spicy shrimp soup called *tom yam goong*. It is made of limes, mushrooms, lemon grass, chillis and garlic with shrimps (prawns) added, and its hot, sour taste is very popular.

Healthy eating

Generally, little fat or oil is used in Thai cooking, which makes for healthy eating. Vegetables are usually stir-fried or eaten raw, including bamboo shoots, bean sprouts, cucumber, lettuce, mushrooms and even the morning glory flower, which is fried and eaten with gravy. Many tropical fruits are available, including bananas (often cooked), guava, lime, mango and papaya (pawpaw). Less well-known fruits include the rambutan (a small, rough-skinned fruit with sweet white flesh) and the durian, which is a large, green, spiny-skinned fruit with strong-smelling yellow flesh that people either love or hate!

Dance-drama

Since ancient times in Thailand, stories have been acted out on special occasions in rich dance-dramas that included music, acting, mime and dance. The stories came long ago from Indian **Hindu** religious tales, but were adapted by the Thais to become popular folk tales. The three main styles of dance-drama are the formal *khon* masked performances, the *lakhon* and the *li-ke* folk theatre.

Khon *and* lakhon

Khon dance-drama began at the royal court of Ayutthaya in 1431 when the Thais invaded the neighbouring Khmer kingdom (known today as Cambodia). Angkor, the Khmer capital city, was renowned for its cultural brilliance, and especially for the grace and skill of its royal dancers. The conquering Thais kidnapped the Royal Dance Troupe and brought them back to the capital, Ayutthaya, for the king's entertainment. In *khon* theatre, scenes from the ***Ramakian*** (religious legends) are acted out with a combination of dance, spoken words and a traditional orchestra. A narrator (the *khon phak*) or a chorus tells the story accompanied by actors who wear elaborate masks and costumes. Characters include the God-King (Rama), the Demon-King (Thotsakan) and the comical Monkey-Soldier (Hanuman). Dance movements are strictly controlled and every gesture has a specific meaning. Vigorous acrobatics are also a feature of the dance-drama. Performers train from early childhood and it takes ten years to master the skills.

Lakhon is a less formal version of *khon* dance-drama. There are two forms: *lakhon-nai* uses the same costumes as *khon*, but most characters do not wear masks. Stories come from **Buddhist** legends as well as the classic Thai epic, the *Ramakian*. The dance movements are generally slower and more graceful, reflecting *lakhon-nai's* origins as an all-female dance performed for royalty. *Lakhon-nork* is a popular form, with male and female performers acting out folk tales for the common people.

A *khon* performance consists of a combination of dance, spoken words and a traditional orchestra.

Wai Kru Day

Performing arts teachers are honoured in a ceremony specially dedicated to them. On *Wai Kru* Day, a white-robed teaching master calls the gods to share a feast. A traditional orchestra (*pii-phaat*) plays, and offerings of food are made to a statue of **Buddha**. A lit candle is handed around in a **ritual** that includes every pupil as they join to pay respects to their teachers.

Li-ke

Li-ke (also *likay*) folk theatre began around 1850 in southern Thailand as a comic version of the very formal *khon* dance-dramas. It combines **pantomime**, dance, music, comedy, acting, folk opera, comments on current events, and lots of interaction with the audience. Characters are not masked and wear outlandish costumes and make-up. Main roles are often played by men dressed as women. *Li-ke* is enormously popular today and is performed as street theatre at fairs and festivals.

Puppets

In Thailand, as elsewhere in Asia, puppet shows are not just for children, but are an ancient and important tradition. *Nang* is puppet theatre in which flat puppets made of leather are held behind a lit screen so that their shadows appear to the audience. It was brought to Thailand centuries ago by the Malays. Today, there are two types of *nang* performed in Thailand. In a *nang thalung* performance, the puppeteer works several small puppets from below by means of long sticks attached to the arms. Stories are from the *Ramakian* and folk tales. Performances can last all night and are a great social occasion for the whole community.

The Thai royal court developed its own version of shadow-puppet theatre called *nang yai*. *Nang yai* is similar to *nang thalung* but the puppets are much larger at around 2 metres tall, and the puppeteer is visible to the audience. Some believe this is a very ancient form of drama from which the *khon* and *lakhon* dance-dramas originated.

Doll-like marionette puppets were introduced to the royal court by the king around 1860. These large, beautifully made wooden puppets are known as *hun*, and are worked by wire rods from below. Few *hun* masters are left to work them but the original royal set of *hun* puppets has recently been restored, and interest in them has revived.

Traditional music

Thai traditional musical instruments are mainly strings (plucked like guitars and bowed like violins), wooden pipes, drums and gongs. Players usually sit on the floor and play by ear, as the music is not written down. There are many different rhythms and sounds layered in the music.

A traditional orchestra (*pii-phaat*) consists of up to 20 musicians who play instruments such as the *pii* (a reed pipe), the *phin* (a guitar-like instrument), the *ranaat ek* (a bamboo xylophone) plus drums and gongs. The main beat is kept by a musician playing the *ta-phon* (twin hand drums), and players offer **incense** and flowers to this instrument before each performance. Originally developed for royalty, *pii-phaat* orchestras are heard today at weddings, festivals, temple **rituals** and traditional sports events.

Thai musicians playing a range of traditional instruments.

Folk and country

Folk music is music originally played and sung by ordinary country people. Many different types of Thai folk music exist but the most famous is *moh lam* from Isan province, in the north-east. *Moh lam* involves song-like storytelling performances, which sound a bit like yodelling. Originally performed at funerals, over hundreds of years *moh lam* developed into a popular folk-singing style. The lyrics usually tell sad tales set in the countryside. *Moh lam* singers are often accompanied by a *kaen*, a bamboo mouth organ. Today, a modernised version of *moh lam* (sometimes backed by electric guitar or a band) is very popular, and albums in this style are big sellers.

Loog thung means 'child of the rice fields' and this is what Thais call their version of country music. It is influenced by American country and western music but also has a strong Thai flavour with a catchy beat and moody, sad lyrics. *Loog thung* singers have a strong following in Thailand.

Pop music

Thai pop music is a thriving industry. Pop records and CDs of local artists are sold in street stalls and shops all over the country. Pop stars are often also well known as actors, actresses or models. For example, the members of the all-female group Seven are all former models and are also solo performers.

Amita Tata Young (born 1980) was already performing at the age of 12 when she won her first recording contract. Since then, the singer, model and actress has sold 11.5 million records throughout Asia, and won countless pop music awards, including an MTV Asian Music Award for best song in 2002 for her hit single, 'I Love You'. She was also awarded Best Actress in 1998 by Thailand's National Film Association for her lead role in the film *O-Negative*. Tata Young's TV soap series, '*Plai Tien*' (White Elephant), drew the largest viewing audience in Thai television history.

Carabao

Legendary Thai music group Carabao became famous in Thailand in 1981 with their hit album 'Made in Thailand'. Their music blends Thai folk with modern rock sounds and lyrics with a strong social, political and conservation message. Carabao is Thailand's most popular band of all time and has a huge following around the world.

Thongchai 'Bird' McIntyre is a pop, film and television star.

Another Thai megastar is the legendary Thongchai 'Bird' McIntyre (born 1958). He shot to fame as a singer with his up-beat hit single, 'Bird Chilli' ('*Prik Kee Noo*') in 1991 but he had been a film and television star in Thailand since 1983. P'Bird, as he is known, is so popular that when he entered a remote Chiang Mai **Buddhist** monastery for a two-month stay as a monk, thousands of fans blocked the road and surrounded the building.

LITERATURE

Classical literature

Long before they were written down, Thai folk tales and stories about the king and his court were told at festivals and gatherings. Stories were filled with magic, fantasy, supernatural beings, love, wars and adventure. Tales called *jataka*, about the lives of the **Buddha**, were written down by scholars around 400 years ago.

Scenes from the classic religious stories called *jataka*, painted on a temple mirror, show episodes from the lives of the Lord Buddha.

The national epic

The best-known story in Thailand is the **Ramakian** ('The Glory of Rama'), based on the famous Indian epic story, the *Ramayana*, about the Hindu gods, but adapted into Thai folklore. This epic adventure was first written in Thai as a long poem by King Rama I (1782–1809). It tells how the villain Tosakanth (or Thotsakan) steals away Rama's wife, Sita, and how Rama gets her back again with the help of the mischievous monkey-god Hanuman. Thailand's famous *khon* dramas and shadow puppet plays draw their stories from the *Ramakian*.

Royal writers

One of Thailand's best poets was King Rama II who, with Sunthorn Phu, wrote the great classic novel, *The Story of Khun Chang and Khun Phan*. His father, Rama I, created the first written version of the epic poem *Ramakian*. More recently, the late Prince Prem Purachatra, using the pen name Prem Chaya, devoted his life to translating great Thai literature into English.

The people's poet

Thailand's most popular poet was Sunthorn Phu (1786–1855) who, after many misfortunes and wanderings, became official poet to King Rama II. He wrote the famous verse-story *Phra Abhai Mani*, a great adventure about two princes' encounters with magical sea creatures and beautiful princesses. This poem has 30 000 lines in 94 books and took 20 years to complete. Sunthorn Phu has a festival dedicated to him in his home town of Ban Kram village and is listed as an '**eminent** classical poet' by the United Nations Educational, Scientific and Cultural Organisation (**UNESCO**).

M. R. Kukrit Pramoj pictured here in 1979.

Man of many talents

M. R. Kukrit Pramoj (1911–1995) is greatly admired in Thailand. This multi-talented man wrote the novel *Four Reigns* (*Si Paendin*) (1953), which traces the modernisation of Thailand. It is enjoyed for its liveliness and wit, especially in its female characters, and its historical settings. In addition to his writing, Pramoj also served as Thailand's Prime Minister in 1975–1976 and founded the Bangkok daily newspaper *Siam Rath*. He even acted in the Hollywood film *The Ugly American* with Marlon Brando!

Twentieth-century works

Prince Arkartdamkeung Rapheephat (1905–1931) caused a sensation in Thailand with his first novel, *The Circus of Life* (*Lakon Heng Tchiwit*) in 1929. It tells of a young law student abroad, his dashed hopes and failed romances. The book was a best-seller, but Rapheephat, a gambler, killed himself in despair at the age of 26.

A much-loved modern classic is *An Elephant Named Maliwan* (*Plai Maliwane*) by Thanorm Mahapaoraya (1908–1961). Her sad and funny tale about a drunkard, his son and an elephant is studied in schools all over Thailand.

Kampoon Boontawee (born 1928) was born to a poor family. Unlike many Thai authors, he writes about everyday people working hard to survive. His novel, *A Child of the Northeast* (*Luk Isan*) won the South-East Asian Writers' Award in 1979. Boontawee was the first Thai author to be given this honour. Another Thai author, Chart Korbjitti received this important award twice for his novels *The Judgement* (*Kampipaksa*) in 1982 and *Time* (*Wela*) in 1994, which are considered modern Thai classics. He also writes film scripts and his work has been translated into several languages.

ARTS AND CRAFTS

Artistic traditions

Sculpture and architecture are the main traditional art forms of Thailand. Throughout Thai history, many different cultural and **ethnic groups** have influenced art styles. Much magnificent artwork in the old capital of Ayutthaya was destroyed in the Burmese attack of 1767. Traditional artists and sculptors aimed to make perfect copies of existing works and styles, using ancient techniques.

Handcrafts such as wood carving, metalwork, weaving, embroidery, basketry, **lacquer** ware and pottery are highly developed in Thailand and provide employment for millions of people, especially in **rural** areas of the north.

Traditional wall painting

Painting **Buddhist** scenes is a holy act in Thailand, so every *wat* (Buddhist temple) is decorated with traditional murals (wall paintings). Mural painters must follow strict rules, including where particular images are placed on the walls. Religious figures and scenes are painted as if seen from above, and are always shown with the same poses and expressions. Natural dyes like **indigo**, white clay and soot were traditionally applied on a layer of paint made from chalk and water. Paintings using this technique eventually faded, and very few murals exist from before the 1800s.

Traditional murals in a Buddhist temple – indigo, white clay and soot applied on a chalk wash.

The father of Thai modern art

A new style of art was established in Thailand by Italian artist Corrado Feroci (1892–1962), who later changed his name to Silpa Bhirasri and became a Thai citizen. He arrived in Thailand in 1923 to teach art, and soon drew praise for his life-like sculptures. He became very popular as a sculptor of images of the rich and famous, including the King, and as the designer of many monuments, including Bangkok's massive *Democracy Monument* (1940), which celebrates the arrival of democracy in Thailand in 1932. Bhirasri established the first Thai School of Fine Arts in Bangkok in 1933. He is now honoured with an official Silpa Bhirasri Day every September.

National Artist

Chakrapan Posayakrit (born 1943) studied under Silpa Bhirasri. He is best known as a realistic portrait painter, although he also paints scenes in the traditional style, including a famous series of 33 paintings on the life of **Buddha**. His painting and drawing style, which blends modern colour techniques with ancient Thai themes, has made him very popular with the royal family. He has painted many portraits of the King and his family. He also renovated the famous royal puppets (marionettes) for the National Museum in Bangkok. In 2000 the government awarded him the title of Thailand's National Artist.

Sculptor Montien Boonma's work *Lotus Sound* uses dozens of silent temple bells to express his Buddhist faith.

Cutting-edge art

World-famous sculptor Montien Boonma (1953–2000) pioneered contemporary art in Thailand. Boonma's work surprises many who see it. His **installations** use simple, local materials such as leaves, beads and spices as well as wood and metal. His works express a strong Buddhist spirituality in a very imaginative and unusual way. *Lotus Sound* (1992) consists of a carefully stacked half-circle of bells with gold-painted wooden droplets mounted above it. His exhibition 'Marks of Mind' (1994) earned him international praise, although his modern style was not as popular in his home country.

Woodcarving

Two thousand years ago, **Tai** tribal people carved beautiful wooden gables for their houses and temples. The tradition is still strong today, especially in the northern forest provinces. The men do the heavy carving with a mallet and chisels, and the women do the fine decorating and sanding. Incredibly detailed and complex teak woodcarvings can take a year to complete.

Mother-of-pearl inlay

Thais have perfected the art of embedding pearly shell fragments into dark timber. The technique is called *krueng mook* and it takes much skill and time. Traditionally used on temple doors, windows and **Buddha** images, *krueng mook* has been used in Thailand since the 700s. The shell of the flame snail (*muk fai*) is shaved to expose the pearly inside, and then cut, sanded flat and carved into tiny pieces. These are glued onto wood to form patterns or scenes, and the areas between are filled with **lacquer**. It is then polished to bring out the multi-coloured shine. The soles of the feet of the famous sculpture of the *Reclining Buddha* in Bangkok are inlaid with 108 tiny designs.

Detail of magnificent mother-of-pearl inlay work on the soles of the feet of the *Reclining Buddha* in Bangkok.

Thai Silk Company

An American, Jim Thompson, helped to revive the Thai silk-weaving industry after World War II. In 1948 he set up the Thai Silk Company in Bangkok to weave top-quality silk for international buyers. His business took off when he was asked to supply costumes for the 1950s Hollywood hit musical, *The King and I* – a film about an English governess who comes to teach the Thai king's children. Queen Sirikit also supports the industry with her organisation, Support, founded in 1976 to promote the hand weaving of silk. Textiles are Thailand's largest export.

A niello-ware silversmith. First made in Thailand around 1400, this metal craft became a sign of wealth and status. Niello ware gifts were sent to Queen Victoria in the 1800s.

Metalwork

In the 1500s, the goldsmiths of the old capital city Ayutthaya dazzled European visitors with their jewellery, made using a technique called filigree. Fine gold wire is spun into exquisite designs of flowers and patterns. Today, the goldsmiths of the town of Phetchaburi turn Thai gold into beautiful filigree jewellery that is worn around the world.

Chiang Mai has been a centre for silver since 1284 when 500 Burmese silversmiths took refuge there from Mongol invaders. Flowers, flame patterns, **Buddhist** images and Chinese zodiac symbols, such as the ox, tiger and rabbit, are still popular decorations for the many silver objects made there today.

Niello ware is a striking form of decoration for metal bowls, plates and furniture. A design is engraved onto gold or silver, and the grooves are filled with a black glossy mix of lead, copper and silver. The resulting pattern does not wear off and objects made using this technique are highly prized. The royal throne in the Grand Palace in Bangkok is decorated with niello ware.

The world's largest umbrella

The village of Borsarng, in Chiang Mai province, is famous for umbrella making. Legends say a monk brought the skill back from a journey to China 200 years ago. Umbrellas (rom) are handmade from bamboo frames and covered with cloth or paper, then painted and lacquered. Borsarng villagers made the world's largest umbrella for the 1996 South-East Asian Games held in Chiang Mai. The annual Borsarng Umbrella Festival is held each January.

29

GLOSSARY

AIDS Acquired Immune Deficiency Syndrome – a fatal, infectious disease caught by blood, or other body fluids, from an infected person getting into another's bloodstream

ancestors people from whom one is descended

artisans artists and craftspeople

batik decorative fabric created by painting patterns onto cloth with melted wax, dyeing the cloth, then removing the wax

betrayal broken trust

Buddha, the founder of the Buddhist religion, Gautama Buddha, or any depiction of him, such as a statue

Buddhist/Buddhism having to do with Buddhism, or a person who follows the Buddhist religion. Buddhism is a belief system originating in India and now practised worldwide, though primarily in Asian countries and cultures. Buddhists follow the teachings of the Buddha and strive for a peaceful state called enlightenment.

censored removed something (especially from a work of art or a piece of writing) because it was considered inappropriate or not acceptable in some way

colonised taken over by a foreign country

compulsory required, often by law

conch shell large shell that can be played like a trumpet by blowing into it

conservation preservation and protection, especially of nature

corrupt dishonest; tending to behave immorally or illegally, especially for personal gain

deadpan showing no emotion or expression

dialect language that is unique to a specific place or area, often a variation of a language that is much more widespread

diverse varied

dominant having power over another group or person

eminent of high rank, distinction or reputation

ethnic group people who share a specific culture, language and background

hardwood durable timber highly prized for making furniture

Hindu/Hinduism having to do with Hinduism, or a person who follows the Hindu religion. Hinduism is an extremely diverse religion that originated in India, in which followers worship many gods and believe in the rebirth of souls into new bodies after death.

hemp plant with tough fibres that can be used for making cloth

incense substance that makes a sweet smell when burned

indecency inappropriateness

indigenous   native to a country or region; original inhabitants

indigo   blue dye made from the indigo plant

inherited   received from older relatives after they die

installations   sculpture-like structures created by artists

jataka   stories about the lives of the Buddha

karma   force that causes deeds performed in this life to affect the quality of the next. The belief in karma is important in both the Buddhist and Hindu religions.

lacquer   shiny varnish for coating wood or metal

merit   reward earned for good deeds

minorities   ethnic groups whose members make up a small percentage of the total population in a region

Muslim   having to do with Islam or a person who follows the religion of Islam. Muslims worship a single god called Allah and follow Allah's teachings, which were spread by the prophet Mohammed and are written about in a holy book called the Koran.

nomad/nomadic   tribal people who roam from place to place; without a permanent dwelling

pantomime   kind of play, usually with singing, dancing and clowns

parliament   group of elected officials with the power to make laws for a country

peninsula   thin strip of land projecting from the mainland

polystyrene   artificial, lightweight foam

Ramakian   a set of ancient stories that have influenced traditional Thai arts, providing characters, plots and themes for dance, drama and artworks. It is a version of the Indian *Ramayana* epic – stories about Hindu gods.

restraint   self-control

retro   style imitating the fashion of the 1950s and 1960s

ritual   traditional religious or spiritual ceremony

rural   located in the country, not in the city

satire   anything that criticises something or someone, often in a humorous way

status   level in society

Tai   tribal people – some still in China – who formed the country of Thailand

tolerance   acceptance of different ways and beliefs

UNESCO   United Nations Educational, Scientific and Cultural Organization; UNESCO belongs to the United Nations system. Its aim is to foster international cooperation in the areas of education, science, culture and communication.

welterweight   middle- or medium-weight category in boxing competitions

INDEX